SECRETS
OF THE
SUPER ATHLETES

FOOTBALL

Abbot Neil Solomon

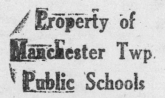

LAUREL-LEAF BOOKS

LAUREL-LEAF BOOKS bring together under a single imprint outstanding works of fiction and nonfiction particularly suitable for young adult readers, both in and out of the classroom. Charles F. Reasoner, Professor Emeritus of Children's Literature and Reading, New York University, is consultant to this series.

Published by
Dell Publishing Co., Inc.
1 Dag Hammarskjold Plaza
New York, New York 10017

Produced by Cloverdale Press, Inc.

Designed by Jon Dewey

Cover photo by Walter Iooss Jr./SPORTS ILLUS- TRATED

Interior photos courtesy of WIDE WORLD PHOTOS

Laurel-Leaf Library® TM 766734,
Dell Publishing Co., Inc.
ISBN 0-440-97979-X
OPM
Printed in the United States of America

BOOK CLUB EDITION

First Printing—August 1982

Fourth printing—September 1983

To MANTICORE, the world's greatest intramural team.

Acknowledgments

This book would not have been possible without the generous help of Frank Ramos, Director of Public Relations for the New York Jets, and his aide, Donna Janoff. In addition, I'd like to thank Paula Vogel from Wide World Photos, Inc., for her assistance and moral support.

CONTENTS

INTRODUCTION

Football is a game of strategy and surprise, tension and high emotion—from the opening kickoff until the final whistle. While the players are on the field, coaches are busy on the sidelines executing their game plan; reacting and responding as the play develops.

Since a pro football team plays each Sunday during the regular season, the remaining six days of every week are crammed with planning and preparation for the next game. Every day of the season is filled with football. Daily workouts are combined with analysis sessions and meetings between scouts, coaches and players. The result is a new game plan for the coming contest.

When game time finally arrives, the offensive team does its best to move the ball down the field into enemy territory —to put points on the board. The defense works to hold back the opposition's offensive drive.

At the line of scrimmage where team meets team—body meets body—the margin of victory is often that special knowledge that a well trained, observant player carries in his head. A linebacker who has studied the opponent's offensive set-up carefully—who knows their moves—can slip into the wide receiver's path and pick off a pass. A quarterback who knows how to "read" a blitz can use that knowledge to score a quick six points by flipping a short pass to an open tight end.

Football is a complicated game. By sharing in that special knowledge—the secrets of the super stars—any fan can get behind the scenes, follow the game with better understanding, and truly appreciate a championship team's long hard journey from the season opener to the Super Bowl.

STARTING LINEUP

The NFL season begins in September on television only. All the players and coaches that make up the 28 teams know too well the August afternoons of action packed competitive practices in the grueling summer heat. It is during this time when the team rosters are made final for the upcoming NFL season.

Minnesota Viking coach Bud Grant, a well respected veteran, opts to hold off a bit. "We're usually the last to get rolling. Championships are won in December, not August. A coach will never forgive himself if a key player gets injured during a rough practice and, as a result, is out for half the season. Now that doesn't mean we goof off during the summer. Believe me, my players hit during preseason too; just ask them."

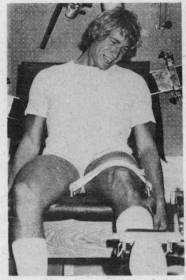

New York Jet quarterback Richard Todd tests leg strength and endurance.

The Pittsburgh Steelers, a dynasty during the 1970's, won four Super Bowls. They owe much of their success to the coaching staff who had a terrific talent for drafting players like Lynn Swann, Jack Lambert, John Stallworth, and Mike Webster. Before the draft, the Steelers had used a complicated scouting system to pick these future superstars out of hundreds of college players. Soon other teams around the league began using the Steeler system. "We're victims of our own success," said coach Chuck Noll about the even quality of recent drafts. "After everyone else saw our success, they began to put more emphasis on scouting. They are drafting better, so it's more difficult to find a Stallworth in the fourth round like we did."

Once the players survive the cuts, their next goal is to become a starter. Each player is assigned a position on a "depth chart"—a list of starters and then the order of substitutes. A Number 2 fullback on the depth chart will start only if the Number 1 fullback is injured or demoted.

Many head coaches like to create competition between players for the starting positions. Former Baltimore Colt coach Ted Marchibroda felt that competition meant better play. "We had a big battle at middle linebacker between veteran Ed Simonini and a second-year man, Barry Kraus. It's a good situation—

Coach Dick Vermeil gets a victory ride, as Philadelphia Eagles' Bill Bergey comforts Minnesota quarterback Tommy Kramer.

a veteran with a kid coming up. I'd like to have it at every position. It makes both players try harder."

Dick Vermeil, head coach of the Philadelphia Eagles, believes that the starting quarterback should learn to handle any situation. "You've got to pick a starting quarterback and go with him. If he's having a bad day, no matter, leave him in. In fact, if you don't, he'll always wonder if he's really good enough. It's on his bad days that he learns how to play quarterback. By fighting his way through mistakes he becomes mature. If a young quarterback is jerked when he's going bad, he'll never fully develop. The only way to handle adversity is to tough it out."

Former Cleveland Browns quarterback Frank Ryan had a similar concept. "The emotional factor in football is so big that you can't win by alternating quarterbacks. It's always harmful to a football player when he doesn't know where he stands. It doesn't matter how much talent he has or how smart he is. He can't play his game unless he knows he's going to be left in the game—even if he makes a few mistakes."

STAYING IN SHAPE

During the heat of summer, while everyone else is basking at the beach, professional football players are getting ready for the season at training camps.

Professional football training camps are well organized. The players live in nearby hotels or college dormitories. After breakfast, the players pick up their gear from the equipment room, then re-

Tommy Nobis working out in the weight
room of the Atlanta Falcons.

port to the practice field and the workout
begins.

Every workout in training camp begins with calisthenics and loosening-up
exercises, led by a team captain or assis-
tant coach. The squads do push-ups and
sit-ups and run in place. Philadelphia
Eagle linebacker Bill Bergey likes the
team workout. "Working out like that
keeps you together as a team. You work
out at the stadium, you razz one another,

you cheer for one another—it's almost like playing a game. When I first came into the league, the weight machines used to gather dust. Now, you have to wait in line to use them."

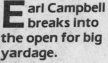
Earl Campbell breaks into the open for big yardage.

After the morning workout, the coaches hold brief squad meetings. Players are able to ask questions at these meetings, and explanations are illustrated on the blackboard.

Earl Campbell of the Houston Oilers works out all year to stay in condition. "I've gotten rid of most of my body fat. I run two miles every day, then do my stretching exercises. Then I have my stomach punched 10 or 11 times, real hard. I want to build up my stomach like a prizefighter's. The stronger my stomach, the better I can absorb the hits in the game."

Kickers use special practice sessions to keep in shape. Some hang a foam-filled bag from the crossbars of the goal-post and kick it to develop quickness. Others practice punting while straddling a long piece of wood to remind them not to cross over their steps. Dave Jennings of the New York Giants keeps his legs in condition by using the leg-lift section of the nautilus. "Some say that weight training for punters reduces flexibility. They say that the best way to condition your leg is to kick 300 punts a day. My leg would fall off."

Football players eat a lot of food to keep up their strength during training camp. In one recent training camp, the St. Louis Cardinals put away 1,360 pounds of steak, 230 pounds of spareribs, 1,200 pounds of prime rib, 950 chickens, 1,200 potatoes, 350 shrimp, 6,000 eggs, and over 300 gallons of milk. These large amounts of food are necessary because a player may lose seven or eight pounds of body weight during a summer practice session.

FORMATIONS
AND
SPECIAL PLAYS

There are three basic offensive formations in football. Depending on the game situation and the types of athletes on the field, offenses in the NFL use the I-formation, the T-formation, or the shotgun.

Until 1940, almost every team had only one offensive formation—the single wing, where the center snapped the ball to a halfback. This formation didn't allow for much variation, and the defense, knowing who would receive the ball, was able to center its attack on the running back.

In 1940, George Halas, coaching the Chicago Bears, devised the T-formation. In this set-up, the center snapped the ball directly to the quarterback, who then had the option of handing off or passing. On December 9, 1940, the Chicago Bears unmasked their new offense and destroyed the Redskins 73–0. The T-formation completely changed the game.

Along with the T-formation, Halas introduced the man-in-motion play. The advantage of the T-formation was that the defense no longer could key only on one back. Sid Luckman, the quarterback for the Bears, said, "The T-formation really shocked defenses. It really spread the defense when Halas put one of the backs in motion."

Hall of Fame guard Danny Fortmann chuckles as he recalls that game against the Redskins. "We scored so many touchdowns that the officials told us to stop kicking extra points after we'd kicked eight into the crowd. They said they'd brought only nine balls and wanted to finish the game!"

Although the T-formation is still used today, most teams have added the I-formation. Houston Oiler head coach Ed Biles describes it. "In the I-formation, the quarterback, halfback, and fullback line up one behind the other. It has its advantages and some drawbacks. The backs are so tight that they can't get outside fast enough into pass patterns to make the formation very effective on passing downs. It limits the play-action pass."

Running back Ricky Bell of the Tampa Bay Buccaneers likes to run out of the I-formation. "The running back is up, not crouched, and he can see the defense. When Coach McKay made that a part of the offense, he said he wanted his backs to see where the holes were. It's great because you can see the defense and what coverage they're going into even before the ball is snapped."

Another formation used in some passing situations is the "shotgun" offense, which was made famous under the direction of Dallas Cowboy coach Tom Landry. In the shotgun, the quarterback is already in the backfield as he takes the snap from center; this lets him see the open spaces without having to

Tampa Bay's running back Ricky Bell breaks a tackle and looks downfield for more yardage.

take time to drop back into the pocket. Other teams, including the Houston

Oilers, have adopted the shotgun. "We decided to use it," says coach Biles, "because it gives an experienced quarterback more time to read the defense and more time to find his receivers. We all know how well it works for Dallas, too!"

The offensive coaches aren't the only ones with special formations. To offset the offense, defensive coaches have devised such key plays as the nickel defense, the blocked kick, and the blitz.

In the blitz, the defensive backfield and linebackers rush the quarterback when the ball is snapped. It puts tremendous pressure on the offensive line and the running backs. Offensive blocking assignments are forgotten as the line tries to "pick up" the charging defensive players. The whole secret of a successful blitz is to make sure the offense is covered. San Francisco 49er defense coordinator Chuck Studley describes their blitz coverage: "If I commit two linebackers to a charge, then I still have one safety who can play free. My two cornerbacks cover the wide receivers, the strong safety keys on the tight end, and my free safety is a stopgap."

"In a blitz, you fight fire with fire," says Giants quarterback Phil Simms.

The blitz can be a costly error if the offense reacts quickly. Long passes can be completed. If the charging defense gets picked up before they enter the backfield, the one-to-one coverage downfield can mean disaster for the defense. Simms continues, "The blitz is a gamble, because it leaves holes in the pass coverage that can be exploited by a quick-thinking quarterback and a running back who can pick up the kamikaze linebacker as he rushes through the offensive line."

Another defense weapon is the nickel defense. (It's called the nickel because five defensive backs are used.) In this defense the fifth back joins the two cornerbacks and two safeties. It's used in certain passing situations. "The real secret to the nickel defense," said Giants head coach Ray Perkins, "is a good pass rush. A strong rush breaks the quarterback's rhythm. He's got to throw the ball too soon or scramble. When the quarterback is pressured or forced out of the pocket, he can't put enough zing on the ball and it can often lead to a key interception. That's what the nickel is all about!"

The kicking teams also have special

plays. One weapon used by a team that's behind toward the end of the game is the "onside kick." It's used after a score to try to get the ball back. Once the ball is kicked 10 yards and is touched, it's up for grabs.

The Minnesota Vikings have a very successful onside kick—they practice them on the day before the game. "Anytime Coach Grant thinks it's worth it, it's worth it," says Viking placekicker Rick Danmeier. Danmeier describes his onside kick: "I cut the very top end of the ball and as it comes off the tee, it'll start to roll end-over-end. The third bounce usually is the high one I want. I practice often enough to get that high bounce."

The defense, too, has its methods to try to block field goals or extra points. When placekickers practice, they sometimes put a volleyball net in front to remind them to get the ball up in the air quickly.

Ted Hendricks of the Oakland Raiders is one of the great kick blockers in the game. "The whole secret is being able to penetrate the offensive line before making your jump. If you can get in and then jump, you cut down the placekicker's angle. It's like a goalie cutting down the shooter's angle in hockey by coming out from the net. My secret is to play behind guys like Matt Millen, John Matuszak, and Howard Long. These guys really put pressure on the line and allow me to penetrate. The kicker is seven yards from the line of scrimmage, so you try to get a quick three or four yard penetration on your rush and then you jump with your arms in the air. The ball usually takes about three yards to get up in the air.''

ON THE FIELD—
THE OFFENSE

THE OFFENSIVE LINE

Offensive linemen are the mystery players of the NFL—operating as a unit and rarely getting the spotlight. They play mostly in an area on the line of scrimmage known as "the pit." The offensive line battles defensive linemen opening up holes for the running backs or protecting the quarterback on pass attempts.

In the 1970's, teams began using complicated blocking assignments for their offensive lines. Today's pro teams use more than 60 different blocking schemes each game. "It's applying the laws of physics to the movement of people," explains Chuck Clausen, line coach of the Philadelphia Eagles. "You have a player with so much power at a certain speed against a player with about the same amount of power and speed. So now it's a matter of applying that force at the best possible angle."

It sounds complicated, but what it means is this: A quarterback needs protection against the defensive linemen in order to pass. The "pocket" for a quarterback used to be an oval-shaped zone made up of offensive linemen back-pedaling and being pushed by the defense. But the new pocket is more rectangular and is made by the center and the guards jamming the play at the line of scrimmage. This rectangular pocket gives the quarterback more mobility when he's looking for an open receiver.

To be a good offensive lineman, a player has to have strength, speed, and intelligence. He has to respond quickly to changing blocking assignments instantly. "They call the offensive line an unskilled position," says Dan Radakovich, offensive line coach for the Los Angeles Rams. "But it takes more skill than any other position in football."

Although the offensive line works as a unit with defined blocking assignments, each of the three line positions—center, guard, and tackle—has its own responsibilities.

The center is responsible for hiking, or snapping, the ball to the quarterback, but he will not survive in the NFL without also learning how to block. His job is extra-hard. First, he must snap the ball, and then set up to block a blitzing linebacker or a charging defensive lineman. Many defenses, such as the Buffalo Bills', put a defensive lineman directly opposite the center. In that case, the defensive man is called the "nose-guard." It takes enormous strength and speed to get the snap off and keep the nose-guard from the quarterback.

On many teams, the center must take charge. During the 1970's, the Miami Dolphins had one of the best centers in the league in Jim Langer. Langer was responsible for calling the blocking signals for the offensive line, and this leadership role was clear in the huddle. According to ex-offensive tackle Norm Evans, "Langer really got us going. He got us pumped up for the battle at the line of scrimmage."

Mick Tingelhoff, who played center for almost 20 years for the Minnesota Vikings, was so psyched he couldn't sleep before a game. "When Sunday came around, I knew it was game day. I'd beat the alarm clock and jump out of bed at 6 A.M.; I was so anxious to get out on the field to play."

No part of the game is practiced more often than the snap by the center. To get a good snap, the center first takes a comfortable stance with his weight evenly balanced. He leans over the ball and maintains such perfect balance that little weight is actually placed on the football. Then he puts his hand on the side of the ball, near the front, with fingers spread around and somewhat under the ball. The other hand, acting as a guide, is placed on the opposite side and near the rear of the ball, thumbs parallel to the seams. As the ball is snapped, both hands must follow through, or the ball will be pulled off line.

A center must be aware of his timing

and snap the ball on the right count. Missing the count will either make his team jump offside or tip off the defense to when the ball will be snapped.

On either side of the center are the guards, who must be quick. Besides protecting the quarterback on passing downs, the guards must be able to "pull" to the outside from their positions to lead blocking on sweeps or delayed plays. The guard must be a more aggressive blocker than the center because on many plays he is called on to continue blocking downfield.

There are two basic plays to any running game: a direct play and the sweep. In a direct play, the running back immediately rushes straight for an open hole in the line. In direct plays, a guard must be able to push back the defensive linemen. John Hannah of the New England Patriots is considered one of the best in the business. At 6'3" and 265 pounds, Hannah explodes off the line of scrimmage and drives his opponent five yards back.

In a sweep, some of the offensive linemen move off the ball laterally instead of straight ahead. The guards pull out and pass the tackles to get in front of the runner and block downfield, moves that require tremendous strength and lateral movements. More than half of the plays in a typical game go toward the sidelines.

Besides being a great straight-ahead blocker, John Hannah is also amazing on the sweep. According to the general manager of the New England Patriots, Bucko Kilroy, "For all his size and explosiveness and straight-ahead speed, John has something most of the others never had, and that's phenomenal lateral agility and balance, just like a defensive back. You'll watch his man stunt around the opposite end of the line and John will stay with him. He'll slide along like a ballet dancer, on tiptoes. And that's a 265-pound man doing that, a guy capable of wiping out an opponent playing him straight up."

The third position on the line is tackle, the spots just outside the two guards. A tackle doesn't have to be as mobile as a guard, and he doesn't need an explosive block like the center. But he must have tremendous strength, because it's his job to hold the defensive line. Marvin Powell and Chris Ward of the New York Jets do such a great job they're called "the bookends."

Offensive tackle Chris Ward of the New York Jets displays a lineman's most valuable weapon.

Offensive linemen study the techniques of the defense before a game and they each have their own method. Doug Dieken of the Cleveland Browns says, "I don't look for a weakness; instead I look for habits or a certain style of play. If I know one guy who responds like some other defensive end I've played against, I'll go back to the game films to see what I used against that other guy."

"During my first couple of years," says tackle Claudie Minor of the Denver Broncos, "I was relying mostly on instinct and size. I was running around like a chicken without a head. The bottom line of all that is that I would get where I was supposed to be, but I would go several places to get there. Now, whatever I do is by plan." He laughed. "I do my homework. A player can improve his game tremendously when he studies."

Offensive linemen have been known to use tricks to stop the defense. Jack Reynolds, a linebacker with the San Francisco 49ers, claims that some linemen are trained to hold a player with the arm that is farthest away from the referee, therefore blocking the ref's view. According to Reynolds, "You have to have agility and speed—but a good strong grip is the next best thing!"

Former Chicago Bears defensive lineman Bill Bishop talks about ex-Packer Jim Parker: "He was one of the greatest tackles in the game. But sometimes he'd get pretty sneaky. Parker would reach out and pull you in and you couldn't get away from him. It looked like he was dancing with you. I often wondered why they bothered to issue him shoulder pads. He rarely had to use them. They should have issued those tearaway uniforms to those of us who had to play against him.''

THE QUARTERBACK

The quarterback is the key man on every team. He's the leader of the offense and usually the club's "star" as well. Even the most casual fan knows Joe Namath, Fran Tarkenton, and Terry Bradshaw.

But because defensive strategies in the NFL are so complicated, it takes time for a quarterback to become a really great player. Every man on the defense is out to get the quarterback and "sack" him. Atlanta Falcon great Steve Bartkowski says, "There's no substitute for experience. Just things like taking the snap, watching plays develop, dropping back and getting hit after you release the ball—that's something you can't teach.''

Terry Bradshaw, who led the Pittsburgh Steelers to four Super Bowl championships, is much more than a great passer. According to teammate "Mean" Joe Greene, "Terry takes command everywhere—on the field, on the sidelines, in the locker room. He wants to win ball games. He pumps everybody up. Terry's at his best now. He's a five-star general. On a team of outstanding foot-

Pittsburgh Steeler quarterback Terry Bradshaw rolls out of the pocket looking for a receiver.

ball players, he's the only guy we can't afford to lose."

"I think I'm a lot smarter now than when I first came up," says Bradshaw. "I can read defenses better, and plan ahead with more confidence. I don't scramble as much as I used to, but by moving around inside the pocket, I'm able to gain more time for my receivers to get open. Even though I can still put some zip into my passes, I rely more on control and the soft touch.

"I've also learned to ask questions in the huddle. I hate to run plays that aren't working, so I'll ask a guy and he'll tell me what he thinks so I can change my plan of attack. Show me a general in the army who doesn't have brains enough to listen to the people out there in the field, and I'll show you a lousy general."

Quarterbacks become team leaders by example. Brian Sipe of the Cleveland Browns likes to take charge. "If anyone is going to take charge, the quarterback is in the position to do it. I don't dwell on it, though. I like to lead by my actions and the guys make it easy for me. I've never concentrated on leadership. It's not a skill you can sharpen."

Fran "The Man" Tarkenton, who

quarterbacked the Minnesota Vikings and the New York Giants during his career, was a field general who wasn't afraid to run with the football. He earned the nickname "The Scrambler" because of that. Ex-Green Bay Packer defensive end Willie Davis describes Tarkenton: "Fran used a mixture of pocket passing and scrambling. But Fran was the type of quarterback who would call his own number in a pressure situation. He was a smart enough runner to avoid a lot of the danger because he'd size up a situation as to whether he could get a first down or not and he'd run to that point. Then he'd head for the sideline and run out of the stadium if he had to avoid a big hit from some charging linebacker."

A quarterback's game plan is often controlled by the head coach. Joe Gibbs, who became the head coach of the Washington Redskins in 1981, put a new passing system in the playbook so quarterback Joe Theismann had to respond. After losing the season opener to the Dallas Cowboys, Theismann admitted that he was still learning the new plays. "Some things came up against Dallas that we hadn't seen before. We're still getting used to our new system."

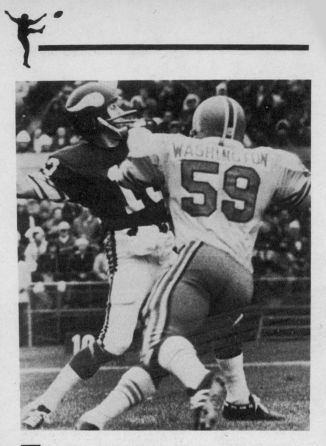

Fran "The Man" Tarkenton rifles a pass downfield.

A quarterback has to be able to quickly forget his mistakes and keep going. "There are three reasons for interceptions:" according to San Francisco's

Joe Montana, "a great defensive play, a bad throw, or a poor decision by the offense." Montana was able to minimize his mistakes in 1981 and lead the 49ers to the playoffs. "Joe's a tremendously resourceful quarterback," said 49er coach Bill Walsh. "When he makes a mistake, he doesn't get too upset and drag it around the field with him. He plays brilliantly."

Experience is the best instructor in the league for quarterbacks. Confidence comes from knowing how to read defenses and waiting for receivers to get open downfield. Craig Morton began his career with the Dallas Cowboys in 1965. Now with the Denver Broncos, Morton has learned a lot over the years. Coach Dan Reeves, an ex-Cowboy himself, praises Morton. "I was a rookie with Dallas when he first came into the league. I once saw him throw the ball so hard that he split the webbing in wide receiver Bob Hayes's hand, between the thumb and index finger. Well, he has really matured. Craig Morton is a player who can do a super job if you give him time to throw. He's been able to sit back and hit the second and third receiver for a first down."

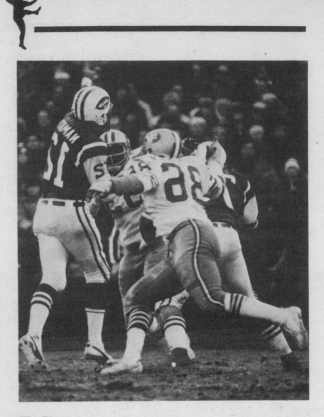

New York Jets quarterback Joe Namath struggles to get off a pass under a powerful 49er rush.

As a rookie quarterback, Phil Simms joined a rookie coach, Ray Perkins, on the New York Giants in the winter of 1979. Simms gains experience with every game. According to his coach, "Phil sees things better now. He anticipates things better. He's better equipped to know where the ball should go, he's sharper. I think he's finally becoming a pro quarterback."

Simms can easily explain some problems he faced during his rookie year. "A lot of what happened was my fault. I know it now. Last year, I might not have been able to accept and admit that. Like when I got sacked 36 times, many of them were my fault. I'd see a linebacker coming in on a blitz and I tried to get rid of the ball too fast. I should have known that a lineman or back was on the way to block. I didn't have the kind of patience I have now. I know a lot more about what the guys are going to do, where they're going to be. You sure learn from your mistakes."

As a young quarterback, Simms doesn't call his own plays. They are sent in from the sideline. "Most times, I'll know what the play is before Coach Perkins sends it in. I know what he's thinking, I know what he wants to do. Sometimes it gets me in trouble, because I see the first few signs from the sidelines [the Giants use hand signals to call in the

plays] and I say, 'Yeah, that's the play.'
But then I turn my back and what
started out as the play I expected turns
into something else.''

Perkins will eventually let Simms
call his own plays. ''When he's ready,
he'll call his plays. He's a quick learner,
and he never makes the same mistake

Dan Fouts fires a pass under extreme pressure before getting hit by Rams' defensive tackle Larry Brooks (90).

twice. There is no doubt in my mind that he is going to be a superstar."

One of the best quarterbacks in the league is Dan Fouts of the San Diego Chargers. As a ball boy with San Francisco in the late 1960's, Fouts used to play catch with the 49er quarterback, John Brodie. "Even then, we would always comment on how tough he was," said Brodie.

Bill Walsh was the quarterback coach at San Diego before he became the head coach at San Francisco. "One outstanding quality Fouts has is keeping calm under pressure. He can concentrate downfield under a pass rush better than any quarterback in the game. The only thing that he needs work on is his footwork. He has to move and keep his feet in balance, which is important to a quarterback so he doesn't get locked into the ground and stand still for very long. A quarterback who plants and waits has a hard time altering his decision to throw to another receiver. When he is facing one way and finds a second receiver on the other side of the field, he can't throw accurately."

A short dropback to pass is one of Fouts's secrets. According to Reggie

Kinlaw of the Oakland Raiders, "Fouts has a short drop of three to six yards and it makes it tough for the defenders to get to him, especially the ends circling from the outside."

Fouts gives a lot of credit to his offensive line. "I'd be dead without those big horses up front. Quarterbacks get a lot of credit when things go good and a lot of blame when things go bad. When I am out on the field, I am playing for my coaches, my family, my teammates, and myself. If I get respect from the teams we play, that is important to me. Winning is the big thing. If you win, everything else follows along."

THE RUNNING BACK

The run is a crucial weapon in any offense. Versatile running backs such as Walter Payton and Tony Dorsett can catch passes as well as run for yardage, thus establishing a glamour position for themselves.

One of the super backs is Earl Campbell of the Houston Oilers. Campbell's combination of speed and awesome strength is often compared to Larry Csonka's, who ran for the Miami Dolphins in the 1970's. Baltimore Colt linebacker Ed Simonini played against both of them. "I'd much rather go against Campbell. When Campbell carries the ball, I usually don't get close enough to him to be run over. Csonka was slower

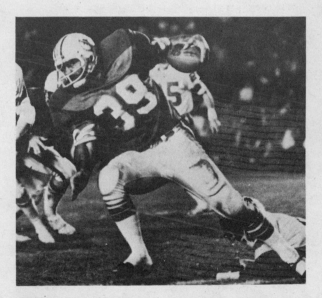

Miami Dolphins' Larry Csonka fights off tacklers to break through for extra yardage.

and unfortunately I got in his way, which wasn't a smart thing to do."

Like all great running backs, Earl Campbell keeps improving. "Earl just keeps getting better," says ex-Oiler coach Bum Phillips, now with New Orleans. "He reads blocks better now. He makes sure to read the keys from the blocking linemen. In his first year, he had a tendency to jump in there too quickly. He'd just try to run over people. Now he probably doesn't punish as many people. What impresses me is the fact that defenses gear up to stop him and he still gets his yards."

Ed Biles is Earl's present coach with the Houston Oilers. "Because of Earl, the offense is able to control the ball more and it gives our defense time to rest and be fresher in the late stages of the game."

Dallas Cowboy safety Cliff Harris has great respect for Campbell. "He's the greatest running back in football. All you can do is close your eyes and hope he doesn't break your helmet."

San Francisco 49er linebacker Jack Reynolds adds that "Campbell can get the yardage when it isn't there...his strength is unbelievable. Earl is special ...he can do anything he wants to do."

Superstar Tony Dorsett breaks loose from Los Angeles Rams' safeties Nolan Cromwell (21) and Johnnie Johnson (20).

Tony Dorsett of the Dallas Cowboys uses his speed to turn the corners and get past the defense. Unlike Campbell, who can blast open holes, Dorsett picks up any opening and heads for it. He's also become a great pass receiver. "I like to have the ball. I don't believe that using a back at only 50 percent of his potential will prolong his career. Any play, whether you're rested or not, can shorten or end a career."

A good example of the modern running back is Billy Sims of the Detroit Lions. Sims prides himself on being a good runner. "I don't avoid tacklers, I look for them. It's the best way to get them to remember you...hit them before they can hit you. I know where all the defensive players are when I start running. I know which ones have an angle and which ones don't. The ones without an angle...man, they'll never get to me."

At 5'11" and 208 pounds, Sims is powerful enough to explode into the secondary when running the ball, but he can still come out of the backfield to receive passes. "I was surprised at the number of times I had to catch the ball. A good running back needs speed, elusiveness, good vision, and good hands," he says.

Miami Dolphin head coach Don Shula appreciates the new pass-receiving running back. "There will always be a major place in a team's attack for a back like Campbell; but moving the ball quickly without losing balance in your offense is the idea now. Anyone will take a back who can average five yards a shot, but most backs can't do that. Throwing the ball is in, and the running back who can catch the ball like Dorsett or Wilbert Montgomery of the Philadelphia Eagles, on a screen or flare is what we want."

The Minnesota Vikings like to pass to their young running backs Ted Brown and Rickey Young. "We just take what the defense gives us," says Tommy Kramer, the quarterback. "When the defense starts covering our short stuff, we air out to Ahmad Rashad and Sammy White."

The Vikings live with the pass. Chuck Foreman played for Minnesota from 1973 to 1979. "If you can't catch, don't even bother to come to Minnesota. You can't play here and be a running back unless you can come out of the backfield and catch the ball. Those are the rules."

The Buffalo Bills have a great all-purpose running back in Joe Cribbs. In 1980, only Earl Campbell, Walter Pay-

Wilbert Montgomery leaps to avoid tackle.

ton, and Billy Sims carried the ball from scrimmage more than Cribbs. Very few backs are as versatile. Besides running, he caught 52 passes, returned 29 punts, two kickoffs, and even completed the only pass he threw.

Walter Payton is the Chicago Bears' running game. "To give you an idea of what the rest of the league thinks about Payton," said Minnesota coach Bud Grant, "in our film sessions our defense actually applauded when they saw Pay-

Buffalo Bills' Joe Cribbs (20) breaks into the open for a 16-yard punt return.

ton make some of his runs. He has that quality both as a football player and a human being."

Don Shula says, "You can't leave it to one man to make the play on Payton. He's too gifted. You need gang-tackling and pursuit. They move him around a lot. He's just a tremendous threat. The Bears live off his efforts."

Walter Payton of the Chicago Bears baffles Cowboy tacklers.

Dolphin cornerback Norris Thomas has seen Payton all too much. "To me, he's a combination of Jim Brown and Earl Campbell. He can run over people or run by people. We try to keep him inside, running between tackles, instead of going outside. You can't give him the option to pick holes and go where he wants."

"I don't try to do anything special," says Payton. "We have an offense set up to allow me to pick my own holes in the line. I try to get in the hole that'll put me past the linebackers. Besides, it's a great feeling to pop into the secondary.

"I think the perfect game is one where you make no mental errors, make all the right decisions on your cuts, are perfect in your blocking, and don't drop a pass. It's tough to be perfect, but I'll be satisfied with 95 percent," says Payton with a wink.

THE WIDE RECEIVER

The wide receivers who leap into the air like acrobats to snag a long pass opened up the offense in the NFL. Twenty years ago, the strategy of most teams was to control the ball by running 60 to 70 times in a game, but during the 1960's, coaching staffs started using the pass to score points. By 1970, it was common for a team to throw 45 passes in a game. The game has changed so much that now a running play can be used to confuse the defense. Wide receivers come equipped with blazing speed and sure-grip hands, and offenses are structured around receivers such as Wesley Walker, Lynn Swann, John Jefferson, and Steve Largent.

The success or failure of the Seattle Seahawks often rides on quarterback Jim Zorn's ability to pass to wide receiver Steve Largent. Seattle's offensive coordinator, Jerry Rhome, praises Largent: "I think people who don't respect Steve get burned. They say, 'Let's play him tight,' and then they get burned. His strengths are that he has quickness, is deceptive in getting open, and is extremely precise in running his routes. He doesn't make just one little move, but he'll do whatever it takes to turn you around. He is a very nifty receiver."

Ahmad Rashad of the Minnesota

Vikings is another talented wide receiver. Rashad has the knack for getting open instantly and making catches that break games wide open. "He's smooth, seems to glide over the field," says ex-teammate Jim Marshall. "Even guys he wipes out never seem to feel it. I could watch Rashad play football all day and feel like I accomplished something." O.J. Simpson played with Rashad on the

Philadelphia Eagles' Harold Carmichael breaks away from Lyle Alzado (77) after catching a pass. The catch broke an NFL record for passes caught in consecutive games (106).

Minnesota Vikings wide receiver Ahmad Rashad tumbles into the end zone with a game-winning touchdown pass.

Buffalo Bills. Says O.J., "He's a real operator on the field. You could call him the 'Surgeon General.'"

Another great wide receiver is Wesley Walker of the New York Jets. "Wesley is such a game-breaker—he's quick and he knows when to check off," says quarterback Richard Todd. (A check-off is a play that is changed at the line of scrimmage if the quarterback reads a shift in the defense.) "During the 1981 season, we checked off whenever we saw that they were putting only single coverage on Wesley. He's so fast that even if the cornerback and safety know he's coming, he can blow right past them. I just try to lead the pass into the end zone."

Walker remembers one check-off that worked against the New England Patriots. "Richard went to the line of scrimmage and saw that the Patriots were going to blitz. It meant that a safety was going to be rushing the quarterback, leaving me one less defender to worry about. He checked off and hit me with a bomb, beating one of the better cornerbacks in the league, Mike Haynes."

Bobby Jones, who is Walker's backup, has the chance to see how other teams try to defend against Wesley Walker. "The way Wesley can catch the ball, they try to do everything to take him away from us. They've been kicking him a lot."

One of the league's most underrated wide receivers is Pat Tilley of the St. Louis Cardinals. "They say I'm too small and too slow. Well, I'm as big as Lynn Swann and just as fast. I run the 40 in

4.6.'' Pat Tilley has averaged more than 60 catches a year for the past three seasons. The St. Louis Cardinals have been increasing their use of Tilley in the offense.

Says Tilley, ''The play calling has been good, and I've been hitting the right kind of coverages. Our offense is not designed to throw to one guy, but I'm put in the slot and that guy usually gets single coverage. Anytime you're running against one man, you're supposed to get open. My job is really fairly easy. I've got one or two guys to outmaneuver. The five guys on the line of scrimmage have to block those big dudes, and that's a tough job. All I've got to do is beat one guy and turn around to catch the ball. I'm just part of the whole, a piece of the machinery, that all has to come together with the play to work.''

The Atlanta Falcons have two excellent wide receivers, Wallace Francis and Alfred Jenkins. Wallace Francis perfected his pass-catching by studying some old techniques. ''After the 1974 season, I spent a lot of time studying films of Paul Warfield and Fred Biletnikoff. I also read Raymond Berry's book, *There's a Catch To It.* In the films I noticed that Warfield and Biletnikoff both had the same kind of skip when they caught the ball, something that helped them with their body control. In Berry's book, I picked up a few tips on running routes. In high school and college I never really had a coach concentrate just on receivers, so I felt I needed to pick up a few tips."

Alfred Jenkins has found a way to use a physical disability to aid in concentration. "I'm nearsighted, so when the ball is thrown, particularly the long ball, I have to concentrate extra hard on just picking it up. I can't be worrying about where a defender is or what he is yelling. I tell people this all the time, and no one ever believes me, but the fact that I wear glasses off the field and not on the field helps me to concentrate that extra amount just to see the ball. Strange, but true."

Alfred Jenkins, at 5'9", uses another physical "disability" as an aid. "Actually, there's an advantage to being small in the NFL. I think some guys figure they don't have to hit me too hard to make me go down, so sometimes they seem to ease up just a bit. Other guys figure I'm someone they can really unload on, so

Atlanta Falcons' wide receiver Alfred Jenkins reaches back to make a one-hand grab.

they try to tear me up. But when a player is trying to bury you, sometimes he loses something on his angle and he winds up not packing the kind of punch he wanted."

Jenkins also offers advice to young players who want to be receivers. "I guess the best advice is that when you know you're going to be hit, just pretend you're a wet dishrag and let your body go limp, and don't cringe. It really cuts down on the injuries."

The better receivers around the league usually draw double coverage. Cincinnati Bengal wide receiver Isaac Curtis offers his way of dealing with double coverage. "I draw a lot of multiple coverage. Most of this is out of a zone, with the strength pointed at me. That puts me in heavy traffic sometimes. But I don't mind. If two people are set up to shut me off, it means someone else on our club is open and that helps the team. Sure, I love to catch the ball. I love to beat a cornerback. I love to run. But, if I do my job well enough to help the team score, then I'm happy. The number of catches I make, the yardage, the touchdowns, what good are they if they're the highest in the league and we don't win?"

When a team has two quality wide receivers, the combination sometimes proves disastrous for the defense. Ray Perkins, coach of the New York Giants, had to prepare to face the Green Bay Packers and their receivers John Jefferson and James Lofton. "More often than anyone in the league," said Perkins, "Jefferson has great hands and is going to come up with the football anytime he touches it. Lofton scares me even more because of his speed. I'll tell you how good Jefferson is. When the ball is in the air, he starts laughing and giggling be-

John Jefferson, wearing glasses, cuts downfield after catching a pass.

cause he knows he's going to catch it. If you get a camera on his face just before the catch, I know you'll see a grin!"

The Dallas Cowboys have one receiver they look to when the game is on the line—Drew Pearson. According to Pearson, "The most important thing for a receiver is to concentrate on the ball when it's coming and to watch it all the way down until it's in your hands. It doesn't matter whether you have good hands or bad hands. If you concentrate so much that you don't know or care about anything else, you'll catch that ball."

For Pearson, worrying about the defense is just another part of the game. "As for the defender's footsteps, I really don't hear them. If you happen to get hit extra hard, you pick yourself up and try to put it out of your mind. The whole thing boils down to intimidation. If a back hits you and you show him that he's hurt you and you don't want to come through the middle again...then he's accomplished his goal. The middle is the worst area. That's where you can get cracked really hard. But if that's the place you have to go in order to catch the pass, then you'd better be there."

Running the proper pass pattern is a disciplined exercise for Drew Pearson. "As far as running patterns, I really feel that I am very much a disciplined player. If the play calls for running 15 yards and out, then that's the way I run it. I feel that my biggest asset as far as running good patterns are concerned is that I can control my speed pretty well."

Dallas Cowboy wide receiver Drew Pearson grabs a pass between two Ram defenders.

Pearson has made a science of how to beat a defensive back. "I look at the defender's feet. If it's a deep pattern, I try to get his feet turned when I make my cut, or I try to get him leaning the opposite way that I'm going. But the very first thing I think to do is close the gap between us, which we call the cushion. The faster I close the cushion, the more advantage for the receiver. Once you're on him, the back doesn't know which way you're going. Then he has to come out of his back-pedal earlier and that's when I make my burst.

"There are many backs who don't play as close as they used to," says Pearson. "So with those guys, you have to use a double fake. The first one is to get them committed and to get them to cross their feet; then you can break by them cleanly. Many times, you don't need that second move, unless the cushion hasn't closed. Most important of all is to have confidence in your ability to catch the ball."

THE TIGHT END

The tight ends in the NFL are largely

Oakland Raider tight end Raymond Chester hangs on to a touchdown pass, despite a crushing blow from K.C.'s Tim Gray.

66

responsible for the changes in football strategy over the last decade. So-named because he usually lines up close to the end of the offensive line, a tight end must have the size and blocking agility of a lineman, combined with the speed and good hands of a wide receiver.

During the 1980 season Junior Miller became the starting tight end for the Atlanta Falcons. With the addition of Miller, the Falcons began to win more games. Falcon head coach Leeman Bennett thinks that Miller is the perfect tight end. "He'll thump into the linebackers to clear holes for the running backs or reach out and catch a football in a crowd of defensive backs. He is especially dangerous as a receiver near the goal line." In 1980 Miller caught 45 passes, eight of them for touchdowns. At 6'4" and 235 pounds, Miller is the perfect size for a tight end.

The tight end also has to respond to blitzes by the defense. Lining up on the line of scrimmage, he must block like a lineman before pulling away into his pass pattern. Some tight ends find it easier to operate against a 4-3 defense (four defensive linemen and three linebackers). Ex-Miami Dolphin tight end

Andre Tillman talks about playing against the 4-3. "With a 4-3 defense, it's easier for the tight end because you don't have that one extra linebacker in the middle, where a tight end runs most of his pass patterns. And if there's a blitz on in a 4-3, all the tight end has to do is read one linebacker. But in a 3-4 (three linemen, four linebackers) the tight end has to read two linebackers and make sure both of them are picked up before running out the pass pattern."

One of the better tight ends in the league is Kellen Winslow of the San Diego Chargers. According to wide receiver Charlie Joiner, "I think Kellen has refined the position of tight end. He's the best in the NFL. He can use his 250 pounds to block like an offensive tackle or run like a wide receiver."

Philadelphia Eagle linebacker Jerry Robinson rates the tight ends. "There are some tight ends I have a lot of respect for, like veteran Raymond Chester of the Oakland Raiders. He's one of the reasons they won the Super Bowl in 1981. He's always coming up with the big play that either sets up a touchdown or scores one. But if I were to give one guy credit more than anyone else, it would be Kellen

Winslow. He's got great hands and great speed and he's super-aggressive coming off the line. He also makes it impossible for a linebacker or defensive end. You

San Diego's tight end Kellen Winslow reaches over the shoulder of a surprised Dallas Cowboy cornerback Benny Barnes (31), pulling in a touchdown pass.

can't really get a good hit on him because he comes off the line attacking you. I remember playing the Chargers and I had to cover him in a man-on-man situation. I thought I was doing a fantastic job. Then all of a sudden, the ball goes up, off my fingertips, and he grabs it with two fingers in the end zone. Our free safety, Bernard Wilson, clobbered him, but he held onto the ball—with just his fingers!"

Some teams use a double tight end formation in their offense, which, in short yardage situations, helps in blocking the offensive line. The Dallas Cowboys use the double tight end often. "What the double tight end offense does," says Dallas Cowboy coach Tom Landry, "is force the defense to balance itself. It forces them to guess where the play is going. With one tight end, you are obviously weaker to the other side, and it becomes more predictable that your running game is going to concentrate on the middle or the strong side. With two tight ends you no longer have a weak side and the defense is never sure."

The San Diego Chargers also use a double tight end formation. Kellen Winslow explains the strategy. "Having another tight end in the offense takes some of the pressure off me. If the other tight end lines up on the line of scrimmage, he's a blocking threat in a strong run formation. If two tight ends line up on the same side, it's even a stronger threat. If we both line up on the same side, it forces the defense to adjust to that. Then if I go in motion to the other side, the defense has to decide if the safety follows me or sticks with the other tight end. It gives our quarterback a chance to find a mismatch or a one-on-one situation.''

ON THE FIELD—
THE DEFENSE

THE DEFENSIVE LINE

The defensive team is responsible for one job—holding the opposition to get the ball back for its own offensive teammates. The offensive opponents trying to make their way up the field will first come in contact with the rough and tough defensive line, positioned right on scrimmage, nose to nose with the offensive linemen.

The defensive line must respond quickly to the various offensive patterns. On a run, the defensive line must close the gaps and tackle the running back. If the quarterback drops back to pass, the line tries to bust through for a sack.

A good defensive line is like a solid brick wall. When the line works together as a unit, they receive catchy nicknames —the Fearsome Foursome of the Los Angeles Rams of the 1960's, the New York Sack Exchange of the 1981 New York Jets. The individuals who excel on the defensive line stand out in every game—Lyle Alzado, Deacon Jones, and Randy White. They are big and strong and play to win.

Randy White plays on the outstanding line of the Dallas Cowboys, along with Ed "Too Tall" Jones and Harvey Martin. White's awesome speed for a lineman allows him to follow the progress of each play and make tackles all over the field. In the off-season, Randy White studies karate and judo to gain control over stubborn offensive linemen. "The way the game is going, I had to do something. With the rules now, an offensive lineman can hold you almost any way he wants. The only time they call a penalty is if he actually reaches out and grabs you as you rush past. But if he keeps his hands inside, man, he can clutch and grab all he wants and he'll never get caught. What's frustrating is they've taken away the defensive lineman's main weapon, the head slap, and at the same time, they've eased up on the holding rule. That's not fair. I'm hoping I can use this karate training to keep those guys from putting their hands on me.''

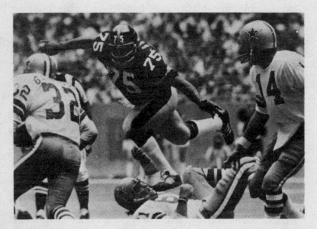

Pittsburgh's "Mean" Joe Greene takes a short cut to halt Dallas Cowboy running back Walt Garrison (32).

Learning to play the defensive line in the NFL isn't easy. "In your rookie year, your reactions are just natural," says Cowboy tutor Ernie Stautner, "because you don't know what's going to happen. In your second year, you're more aware of what's going to happen. You start thinking, but you can't adjust as fast. When you think too much, it slows down your reactions. You have to go through that phase when your natural reactions come back."

Lyle Alzado has been an intimidating force in the league for the past 11 seasons, first with the Denver Broncos and then the Cleveland Browns. Although Alzado is known for being crazy on the field, there's a method to his madness. "The trick to beating me at my own game is to keep away from me. If a running back runs straight at me, no problem...I'll mangle him. Sometimes things get on my nerves, get me upset and angry. When I get mad, I can get so wrapped up in the guy on the other side of the line that I forget my job. I forget the quarterback or even the ball carrier. I guess that's my worst weakness. But I'm still a good player. Sure I'm emotional, but I don't go jumping on top of guys after the

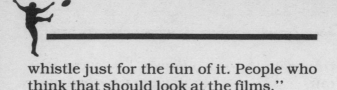

whistle just for the fun of it. People who think that should look at the films."

At 6'3" and 245 pounds, Gary "Big Hands" Johnson is a terror on the San Diego Charger line. Coach Don Coryell says, "He's so fast that on some of his quarterback sacks, he rushed past the linemen so quickly, he was hardly touched."

Johnson prepared himself before every game. "I think about my opponent's style and what I have to do to ruin it. When the whistle blows I'm ready. I'm not a screamer or yeller like some guys. I don't hate quarterbacks...I just don't like them. They're the deadliest enemy on the team. If they're not making you chase them, they're sitting back in the pocket looking pretty and throwing that big pass on you. I don't want to hurt a player. I just want to shake him up, take the gusto out of him."

During the late 1960's, the Los Angeles Rams defensive line earned the title the Fearsome Foursome. Made up of Merlin Olsen, standing 6'5" and 276 pounds; Roosevelt Grier, 6'5" and 296 pounds; Lamar Lundy, 6'7" and 263 pounds; and Deacon Jones, 6'5" and 255 pounds, the Fearsome Foursome destroyed any and all offenses. "We were so tall," said Grier, "that when we stood up at the scrimmage line or went running in with our arms up, the quarterback needed a stepladder to see over us. And we were so heavy that we could flatten a Cadillac if we climbed on the roof."

Deacon Jones was a standout on the Fearsome Foursome. His speed had been clocked 9.8 seconds in the 100-yard dash. During a game against Green Bay, Deacon dropped Packer great Bart Starr for a four-yard loss. "He was in on me so quickly that I thought he was one of my own blockers," Starr said afterward.

Ezra Johnson of the Packers is one of the league's best pass rushers. He gives credit to teamwork for his personal success. "Getting sacks may seem like an individual thing, but teamwork is the most important part. The backs and linebackers have to cover the receivers before the quarterback can pass, and the offensive line has to be doubling up on someone else for me to break through. Sometimes I get through and the passer is standing there with nothing to do. He's a sitting duck."

The San Francisco 49ers made the playoffs in 1981 thanks in part to the play of Fred Dean. Dean has amazing strength for a player who weighs only 230 pounds. "I never lifted weights in my life. My strength is farm-boy strength. I baled hay when I was a kid, hauled logs. And I did some serious eating." Chuck Studley, the 49er defensive coordinator, calls Dean "the most thoroughly dedicated football player I've ever known. He has great speed, so he can attack the offensive backfield before they can get going." Says teammate Archie Reese, "He's got so much speed and balance he could be a fullback if they'd let him play offense." The 49er defensive line acquired a nickname during the 1981 season—"Dean-fense."

Denver Bronco lineman Rubin Carter knows the fine points. "Most people would be surprised at how much faking goes on in the line. Sometimes you might show a blocker your left hand and grab him by the shoulder with your right. Sometimes you fake one way, bring the center with you, and then use his momentum to throw him down or into one of his own players. Occasionally I out-fake one of those fancy running backs. I'll make him think I'm blocked when I'm not, act like I'm out of the play to draw him toward me. Hey, you have to use a little intelligence out there to set people up."

Veteran Jack Youngblood has played the line for the Los Angeles Rams for over 10 years. He owes a lot of his success to the defensive team working as a unit. "Our whole defense depends on everyone doing his job. It takes 11 men working together to make defensive play successful. Anytime I sack the quarterback, it's because the other guys are doing their jobs right."

Youngblood started his career by playing alongside monsters like Merlin Olsen and Deacon Jones. "I learned a lot from the stars. Deacon taught me about playing defensive end in the pros. Merlin taught me to play each play as if it were the only one in the ballgame."

Youngblood tries to analyze his performance after each game. "You try to improve every game. You remember your mistakes and learn to deal with them. A good defensive end is only as good as his last play."

Youngblood makes a careful study of the offensive lineman he'll be playing against each week. "I have to know the moves that the tackle playing against me

L os Angeles Rams' Merlin Olsen takes
down Archie Manning any way he can.

has before I can adjust to the play. The
whole idea is to fight off any blockers,
keep your eye on the ball carrier and
make the play.''

On a pass rush, Youngblood uses his
quickness and skill to get past a blocker.
''It's a three-point approach. I'll put my
face mask against his and my hands on

his shoulders. If he fights the pressure, I'll use his momentum and pull him past me to the side. If he doesn't fight my move to his shoulders, I usually fake one way, and slip past him on the other side before he grabs me. Usually it works and I bust through."

THE LINEBACKER

Powerful linebackers are a must for a strong defensive unit. They must be strong enough to tackle running backs who sprint past the defensive line and agile enough to cover receivers downfield. On most teams, the middle linebacker is the signal caller for the defense.

On the average he is at least 6'2" and 230 pounds and has the agility to spring from one area of the field to another. During practice, a linebacker drills off a blocking sled. With a coach standing on the sled, the linebacker drives straight ahead, pushing the sled with all his might. On a signal from the coach, the linebacker peels off to the right or left as if following after a running back. This drill teaches him to fend off blockers

Linebacker Steve Nelson of the New
England Patriots stops Miami's Nick
Giaquinto.

while stopping the running back.

Steve Nelson of the New England Patriots believes that a linebacker must prove his strength on the field. "If I really pop a back coming into my zone, he'll be looking for me the next time. That'll reduce his concentration on the ball and maybe we can take advantage of it. In training camp we don't hit very much, so I think you really have to start hitting people in preseason games. You have to get a sense of pride in your defense. You really have to hit hard."

Nelson knows the importance of teamwork. He hates a player seeking personal goals at the expense of the team. "To be successful, it takes 11 guys working together to do the job and compete against the other teams. In basketball, you can get a Dr. J. or Kareem Abdul-Jabbar and with that one guy you can have a successful team. But in football, one guy can only get you so far."

Of course if you're a physical hitter like Steve Nelson, the time will come when you're in some pain. "I never like to show I'm hurt. I do get hurt and I don't know if it's my ego or what, but I never want to let the other guy know that he really hit me."

Like Nelson, Eagles linebacker Frank LeMaster loves the contact hit in football. During the 1980 season, LeMas-

Steeler linebackers Jack Lambert (58) and Jack Ham bring down Cincinnati's running back Archie Griffin.

ter totaled 38 initial hits against the run. "It's simple. I want to be the best middle linebacker in football. I've always been a highly motivated person. I love football, therefore I love contact—it's fun for me. I want to dominate. I can stand toe-to-toe with any guard in the league." LeMaster feels that while some linebackers get a big name from the media, "the big image just won't help you on Sunday against veteran players. You might be able to intimidate rookies with the media image, but nothing proves your point more than a crunching tackle."

Jack Lambert of the Pittsburgh Steelers has been referred to as the "Darth Vader" of the NFL. Many rate the aggressive Lambert the best middle linebacker in the game. "Sure, I play active football. But sometimes all the media talk upsets me because I'm not a dirty football player. I don't sit in front of my locker before a game, thinking about getting into fights or hurting somebody. All I want is to be able to play football, hard and aggressively...the way it's meant to be played."

A seven year veteran, Lambert has developed a great feel for the game. "I've seen everything, and I now find myself

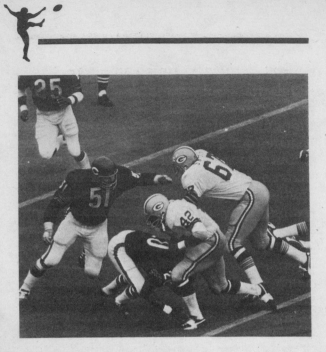

Linebacker Dick Butkus (51) prepares to finish off Green Bay's John Brockington (42).

sensing plays before the ball is even snapped. In a game against Cleveland, we were ready for the run. But on the snap I sensed a quick screen pass. I went with the flow and crossed the line of scrimmage, throwing the running back who had caught the ball for a seven-yard loss. Sure it was a guess, but I don't guess wrong very much anymore."

And then there's Dick Butkus. Ever since he was drafted by the Chicago Bears in 1964, Dick Butkus has been the measuring stick for linebackers. To Butkus, tackling is an art. He talks about the position: "When I was the first tackler, I wouldn't go for the ball. In other words, if I was all by myself, I just wanted to bring the man with the ball down. But if he was coming through the middle of the line and he'd already been hit by two or three other guys, I'd go for the ball. I wanted to strip him down and make him lose the ball. If I could cause a fumble, that took the heart out of the other team."

Stan White, of the Detroit Lions, is responsible for calling the defensive signals. "It's a two-step process. First, I'll call the signal for the defensive line. Then I'll announce the backfield coverage. Before they snap the ball, I'll see who's in motion for them, and if I have to, I'll slap one of my sides to let my cornerback know who to cover."

The New York Giants' Lawrence Taylor spent his rookie year physically telling other teams that he meant business. He is a scary player with amazing

Philadelphia Eagles linebacker Bill Bergey cracks New York Jets' Clark Gaines, forcing a fumble.

speed that makes him a big part of the gang-tackling pursuit of the defense. During his rookie year, he realized the value of putting pressure on the offense. "I love sacking the quarterback. A sack is like a touchdown for the defense. Anytime you get a sack, it turns the momentum toward the defense and forces their offense to go for the big play. This leads to mistakes like interceptions or fumbles."

During the first half of his rookie season, Taylor sometimes was too aggressive and would run by the running backs. "I'm starting to slow down now. Coach Perkins puts in a misdirection play during practice to keep me on my toes. Sometimes I do go in too aggressively. I'm working on slowing down and looking at everything before I go. I'm proud to be playing with guys like Harry Carson, Brad Van Pelt, and Brian Kelley —some of the best linebackers in the business. When people say we have a strong linebacking unit, it makes me feel real good."

THE DEFENSIVE BACKFIELD

The defensive backfield is known as the "last line of defense." Like the goalie in hockey, getting past them means points on the scoreboard. "The only thing between me and six points," says cornerback Gary Green of the Kansas City Chiefs, "is my mistakes and green grass."

Cornerbacks and safeties make up the defensive backfield. Cornerbacks cover the swift wide receivers as they race downfield. The safety acts as a "mini-linebacker," either forcing a run or dropping back to help the cornerback on the pass.

"Playing defensive back today takes a much better athlete than it did 10 years ago," says Lemar Parrish, 12-year veteran cornerback for the Washington Redskins. "There are many reasons: bigger and faster receivers, more varied offenses, and some super quarterbacks who aren't afraid to throw on first down." But the main reason is the "no-bump" rule, which was imposed in 1979. Until then, a defensive back could bump a receiver anywhere on the field, upsetting the timing or pass route of the play. "Before 1979, you could operate with a little less speed and a lot more aggressiveness," says Parrish. "But now, we can bump receivers only within five yards of the line of scrimmage or else it's a 15-yard penalty."

As a play develops, the defensive back has to be ready to adjust to any changes that occur on the field. "When you're out there guarding your own man," adds Parrish, "you've got to be thinking all the time about everyone else. You keep your eye on your man and, in certain situations, on the quarterback as well. You can bet he knows your movements as well as you know the receiver's. If the offensive backfield comes at you, you've got to move up quickly for the ball; if your man switches zones, you've got to watch for another player crossing over the middle to enter your zone, or maybe you should be dropping back to help out the safety. These have to be reactions...there isn't time to really think about what should be the right move."

Oakland Raider cornerback Lester "the Molester" Hayes grabbed 13 interceptions in 1980, one shy of the regular-season record. "Intimidation is a big part of my job, and I do it well."

Lester tells one secret that he uses to fool the receivers. "Sometimes I want the receiver to think that he has me beat. Listen, if a guy is sure he's going to catch the ball, he has to relax a little bit. When he lets down, I'll appear and knock the ball away or intercept it...that'll destroy his confidence."

Part of Lester Hayes's success in

Oakland Raiders' cornerback Lester Hayes applies "stickum" to his hands.

1980 was attributed to use of a substance called "stickum," which he sprayed on his arms and hands. Unfortunately for Hayes, the league banned the use of stickum starting in the 1981 season. "I learned about stickum from former Raider wide receiver, Fred Biletnikoff. The ball always seemed to be glued to Freddie's hands. But what really convinced me how powerful the stuff is was when I saw cornerback Pat Thomas of the Rams shut out Freddie in 1978. Pat was playing him real tight and the stickum Freddie was using on his hands was working against him. Freddie was actually sticking to Pat and it was throwing off his timing."

The man who still holds the single-season interception record is Dick "Night Train" Lane, who picked off 14 passes in 1952 when he played for the Los Angeles Rams. Lane believed that the best way to cover a receiver was to get the proper angle on the play. "My initial position as the play started was very important. You had to have a perfect view of both the quarterback and the receiver, except when our linebackers blitzed. You couldn't look at the quarterback then. He'd get rid of the football too fast. Another big thing is being able to recover. Once in a while a receiver would beat you. But you had to recover...never give up."

Night Train Lane offers another secret about covering a pass receiver. "Watch the belt buckle, the waistline. That was my secret for playing cornerback. Never look at a receiver's eyes. They'll fake you into the stands if you key on their eyes. Just watch the belt

"Night Train" Lane intercepts a pass during the 1952 season. Notice that his helmet didn't have a faceguard.

buckle. His legs aren't going to go anyplace without that buckle."

Despite advice of Night Train Lane, the Dallas Cowboys are taught to watch the receivers' eyes and to ignore the flight of the football. Aware of this coaching theory of the Cowboys, the Minnesota Vikings were able to rally against the Denver Broncos in 1981 by fooling ex-Cowboy cornerback Aaron Kyle. Minnesota quarterback Tommy Kramer threw downfield to receiver Ahmad Rashad. Kyle, who'd been recently acquired from Dallas, was covering Rashad on the play and wasn't looking at the ball. Rashad looked downfield and Kyle broke toward the end zone to cover what he thought would be a long pass. As soon as Kyle took off, Rashad turned around and caught the pass and ran for a big gain.

Louis Wright of the Denver Broncos is a defensive back who checks the quarterback. "I look at the score, who's winning, what down. Sometimes they'll break out of the huddle and I catch the quarterback glancing over at me. When that happens, I get pumped up because I know he's going to pass. Another tip is to watch how the receiver approaches the line before the ball is snapped. Some of them jump over to the line and that often means that he'll be expecting a pass and he's a little anxious."

Cornerback Jeff Griffin of the St. Louis Cardinals feels that intimidation is a big part of his job. "A lot of receivers don't like to get hit. I like to hit them. I punish receivers and point to them and

Denver Broncos cornerback Louis Wright tips a pass away from Giant receiver Danny Pittman.

talk to them. I try to get them thinking about me rather than catching the football.''

Dennis Thurman plays cornerback for the Cowboys. He feels that persistence is the key to the position. ''It's all mental. You're going up against the best wide receivers in football. And they're probably going to beat you from time to time. You just have to be strong-willed. If you worry about getting beat or about what people are going to say about your performance you're in trouble. If a receiver catches a ball, you tackle him. You keep at it in hopes that something will eventually break down and you'll get your chance to make a key interception or knock the ball away."

THE KICKING GAME

The punters and placekickers put the "foot" in football. Positions such as quarterback or running back may get most of the media attention, but the teams with the stronger kicking games are rarely beaten.

During most NFL games, a team will punt an average of eight or nine times. A longer punt puts the opponents in worse field position and makes matters more difficult for them.

The placekickers are responsible for kicking off, making field goals, and kicking the extra point after a touchdown. While the punter need be concerned only with his individual technique, the place-kicker works with the center and the holder. Placekickers and punters play under enormous pressure. In the final minutes of a close ball game the kicker can mean everything.

Punting

The punter has five major concerns. He must: a) kick the ball far, b) get it away quickly, c) make the ball "hang" in the air for at least four seconds, d) aim the ball either toward the corner or away from the punt receiver, and e) be consistent.

Punters usually try to remove themselves from the pressures of game situations, so they can operate smoothly in spite of the urgency of a particular kick. Dave Jennings of the New York Giants is considered the best punter in the NFL. Jennings says that one of the keys to being a successful punter is motivation. "It's pride in wanting to excel and enthusiasm in doing what you have to do to help the team. A punter can't get down on himself."

He adds that, "Punting is such a mental thing. It's the lack of the proper mental attitude that destroys so many punters. You need a special personality or else you can put too much pressure on yourself and it'll destroy you."

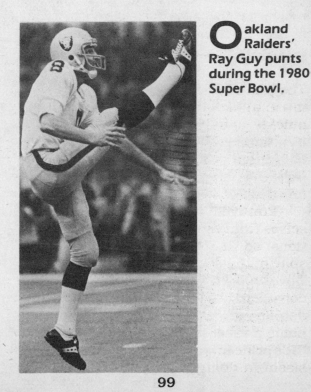

Oakland Raiders' Ray Guy punts during the 1980 Super Bowl.

When the outcome of the game is up for grabs, Jennings prepares. "I pace on the sideline telling myself that I want to kick that football. I love to be on the spot and boom one that'll crush the other team psychologically."

A bad punt can destroy a game or a season in only one play. "I value a great punter," says New York Giant general manager George Young. "If you're going for a championship team, you want an edge that makes you a freckle better than the other guy. A punter is that edge and that's why we hold on to Jennings." The punting game has become so important that punters are often selected in the first round of the annual college draft.

The difference between an established punter and a mediocre punter is execution of the kick. It takes many hours of coaching and practice, as well as the ability to respond under pressure.

"When I first started in the league," says Jennings, "I used to take it easy. Now, I work harder. I probably punt between 75 to 100 balls a day." During practice, Jennings works on his timing and coordination. "The most important elements are the drop and the hit. A punter should hit the ball as hard as possible without upsetting his timing. Guys who try to kill the ball, bending their backs and whipping their heads back are off-balance and that usually means disaster."

To get the best distance on a punt, Dave Jennings follows a well-supported theory. "With the ideal punt for distance, the front end of the ball should tilt up. This keeps it rising and floating. If you let the front end turn over, the ball will drop straight down, shortening the distance."

Over the years, one of the league's best punters has been Ray Guy of the Oakland Raiders. Guy usually checks the wind direction before each of his punts, but in the era of the domed stadium, checking for wind is useless. Playing in Super Bowl XV, Guy was happy that it was played in New Orleans' enclosed stadium. "You don't have to contend with any wind. All you have to do is check to see which way the air conditioning is blowing."

The "coffin-corner" kick, perfected by Jennings, got its name from the fact that if properly executed it buries the other team deep in its own territory. According to Jennings, it's simply a matter of geometry. "You have to kick longer when you're trying to kick one out of bounds. A 30-yard kick angled toward the sideline equals a 45-yarder hit straight downfield. I see the football field geometrically and estimate how much I have to give a punt. If I get a good reading and it is angled right, I can get the ball to drop out of bounds inside the 10-yard line. Once I see it slide out inside the 10, I like to glance over to the player who was expected to make the return. The expression on his face usually tells me that I've done my job.''

Placekicking

The placekicker has become one of the most devastating offensive weapons in football. Placekickers are a lot like relief pitchers in baseball. Both are called into the game in pressure situations and their performance can be the margin of victory. They both must be able to quickly forget any setback in order to be successful in the next attempt.

The placekicker must love pressure. Rolf Benirschke, placekicker for the San Diego Chargers, says that, ''any kicker likes the outcome of the game to come

George Blanda, at 49 years of age, kicks yet another field goal.

down to him. We were playing the Kansas City Chiefs and during the first half I missed an extra point. We wound up trailing 20–19 with only 13 seconds left in the game. I just didn't want it to come down to our losing because of my missed extra point so I hoped to get a chance to win the game for us—and I did. I came in, kicked the winning field goal and was the hero."

Learning to respond under pressure is the key. Joe Danelo is the placekicker

New York Giant Joe Danelo lifts an overtime, game-winning field goal over the blocking attempts of the Buffalo Bills.

for the New York Giants, and during the 1981 season he kicked a clutch field goal in overtime to upset the Dallas Cowboys. "That's my job. Sure I was anxious, but I wasn't nervous or hyper. The tough part is the waiting. Once you're on the field, you feel real good. You calm down."

Like many kickers in the NFL, Danelo likes to practice under simulated game situations. "Our offensive backfield coach, Bob Lord, gives us pressure situations. He might say, 'Two seconds left in the game, we're down by 2. If you don't kick a 40-yard field goal, we lose.' We always have these practice-type pressures, so when we face them in a game, they're nothing new...we've done it before."

Pat Leahy is the placekicker for the New York Jets. He constantly makes adjustments to perfect his kicking form. "I remember being in a bad spell. I was missing a few and couldn't figure it out. I watched a few films and noticed that I was lifting my head to follow the flight of the ball. I saw that by bringing my head up, I wasn't connecting with the ball properly. I made the adjustment and broke out of my slump."

The field-goal-kicking unit practices

during the week to get the timing down perfectly. On most teams, a special long-snap center works out with the team's holder. Usually the holder is a player, such as a second-string quarterback, who is familiar with handling the football. Of course, mistakes can happen. Dan Devine recalls an embarrassing moment that happened when he was coaching the Green Bay Packers. "The field-goal unit spends part of each practice session working together. It's a precision machine. We were playing the Bengals in Cincinnati and there was a field goal situation. We sent in the kicking unit and I began to count the players—one, two, three…we only had nine players on the field! You know who was missing? Only the kicker and the holder!"

The placekicker is also responsible for the extra point after a touchdown. In the extra point conversion attempt, the placekicker must put his foot squarely into the lower half of the ball and lift it more than 19 yards over the crossbar. He must kick quickly to get it up and over a defender who attempts to jump up and block the kick.

A missed extra point is a damaging blow to a team. John Madden was head

Tim Mazzetti follows through on a field goal.

coach for the Oakland Raiders for 10 seasons. "A missed conversion is one of the more painful things to a team that has just scored a touchdown. Somehow a missed extra point always seems to come back and haunt you in the end. It's always in the back of your mind."

One of the more interesting and durable placekickers is Tony Franklin of the Philadelphia Eagles. Tony Franklin never felt comfortable kicking with his shoe on. "One day when I was a sophomore in high school, I took off my right shoe and kicked the ball just to see what would happen. The ball boomed 50 yards and I haven't worn a shoe since. When I kick with a shoe, I feel real brittle and my foot feels too bulky. I don't feel like I'm hitting the ball strongly enough."

To be effective, Tony Franklin must have a feel for the football. "Without a shoe, the feel is everything. And despite what most people think, I don't feel any pain. I'm concentrating, so I don't feel it. Then it stings, but only for a second. Just a little sting and that's it. And the ball still winds up 60 yards away. It's kind of like one of those mind-over-matter things, like when a karate expert splits those cement bricks with his hands."

Tony Franklin also likes to work on his leg speed. "Besides a feel for the football, the next biggest factor is leg speed. And the less weight a leg carries, the faster you can make it go." Franklin has had his footballs timed at 117 miles per hour. "A lot of kickers float the ball... mine explodes."

BETWEEN-GAME
ANALYSIS

Although a football team plays only one game a week, the players follow a strict routine between games. Injuries get constant medical attention. Coaches plan the strategy for the next game. But the most important part of the routine between games is the viewing and analysis of game films.

For this, the team is broken down into defensive and offensive units, and game films from the previous weeks are used to point out mistakes and ways to correct them. As the week progresses the team begins to analyze films of their upcoming opponent. Weaknesses and strengths are pointed out. Blackboard sessions are followed by field practice until the team is comfortable with the game plan for the upcoming game.

The coaching staff, in analyzing the

Coach Vince Lombardi and the Green Bay Packers prepare to study game films.

game films, can spot weaknesses in the defense of the opponent. The Buffalo Bills defeated the Cleveland Browns during the 1981 season with the help of the pass-catching by running back Joe Cribbs. Cribbs caught five passes that day for a total of 163 yards. "It was a situation we saw on the films," said Bills quarterback Joe Ferguson. "They were placing a double coverage on the two wide receivers. When you get Cribbs alone with the linebacker in one-to-one coverage...it's a big mistake."

The films also show trick plays that an opponent uses in certain situations. "We were watching films of the Kansas City Chiefs," said Chicago Bear coach Neill Armstrong, "and we saw that their two best field goal blockers, Gary Green and Stan Rhome, were illegally stepping on the backs and shoulders of the linemen to block kicks. I got word to the officials to keep an eye on it. Sure enough, they called an unsportsmanlike penalty on them and we gained enough yards on the penalty to set up a 22-yard field goal in overtime to win. I've never seen that called before, but we noticed in the films that they had been doing it all season."

Minnesota Viking coach Bud Grant
checks the play charts during practice.

During the week, the quarterback is
under constant pressure to prepare for
the next game. Danny White, quarterback for the Dallas Cowboys, describes
his routine. "The real burden I deal with
is the pressure of performing every
week, playing every Sunday without a
break and trying to maintain a high performance level. If you've been sitting on
the bench for four years, collecting dust,
like I did, it's a hard transition to make.
Once the season starts it's *bang, bang,
bang.* No let-up, no time to sit around.

You get through with one game and it's time to get ready for the next one. You get to the point where you're gasping for air. It seems like I'm always viewing game films. But I couldn't survive without them. The more I can learn about the other team's defense, the better I can use that knowledge to beat them on Sunday.''

Phil Simms, quarterback of the New York Giants, has a disciplined schedule between games. The day after a game, Simms gets up early and goes to the stadium. "I usually get there about 10 A.M. and watch the films of the game. After lunch, I go out to the field and loosen up with the other players for a few hours. Then I like to lift some weights and take a sauna and steam bath before going home. On Tuesday, when most of the team has a day off, I meet with Coach Perkins and we go over the films again. On Wednesday, the whole team practices, watches films, and meets with the different coaches. Wednesday night is a late night because the quarterbacks have extra meetings with the coaching staff. Thursday, it's the same routine... eat, stadium, meetings, practice. It's a regular routine we follow but it's necessary."

Teams also prepare for the type of surface they'll be playing on—natural grass or artificial turf. "Artificial turf makes you faster. I always notice the difference when I play on grass," said New England Patriot defensive lineman Tony McGee. "Since grass is slower and I'm a speed person, I'd much rather play on synthetic turf. On grass, it always takes a few series of plays to adjust."

The artificial turf also affects running plays. Since running backs are faster on artificial turf, many plays are badly timed because the exchange of the football is slightly behind the runner's footwork.

Dr. Steven Tager is an expert on foot problems resulting from artificial surfaces. "In a way, playing on artificial turf is like trying to walk across ice. Since there is less traction with your feet on the turf, players tend to stand higher to keep their balance. On grass, the cleats actually dig into the ground and players are able to keep their balance with a lower stance. So when players move from turf to grass, their bodies have to unlearn everything they've learned and adjust."

INJURIES

In a physical game like football, injuries are common and their prevention and treatment has become an important part of the game. By using scientific data, special programs are developed for particular athletes to prevent certain injuries.

Running backs are famous for knee injuries. Veteran Calvin Hill of the Cleve-

Calvin Hill is helped off the field after injuring his knee in playoff action.

116

land Browns uses daily applications of ice since he tore knee cartilage in 1971. "It's been so long I can't remember what it would be like to play with a good knee. At Yale, I used to long-jump 25 feet off my right leg, but I can't now. I've accepted it and learned to get around the problem. After hurting the knee, I became more aware of what defenders were doing." He has some bone spurs and flaking of the kneecap along with arthritis in the knee. "There is no significant change in the bone structure so I'm not concerned about the future. I've watched the knee carefully and I've made up my mind that even after I'm out of football, I'll still stay in condition."

Cincinnati Bengal offensive tackle Anthony Munoz has had three knee operations, but he has an amazing ability to bounce back after surgery. According to his wife, "After one of the operations, I found him skipping rope on one leg while the other was on a cast. He started running the day the cast came off."

Seattle Seahawk coach Jack Patera has taken a different approach to injuries. He hired Johnny Kai, a retired major in the Green Berets. "My players had lots of injuries last year," said Patera. "Kai sees the players on a voluntary basis and works with the trainers, too. Say a player has a sore calf. The trainer treats him medically, but Johnny teaches him to mentally suppress the pain. It's mind over matter."

The New York Jets team orthopedist is Dr. James Nicholas. Perhaps the best in the business, Dr. Nicholas earned his reputation during the Joe Namath era. He started a procedure where prospective draft choices undergo a series of tests called a "pre-participation profile," which determine the likelihood that a player will get injured because of his physical makeup. Says Dr. Nicholas, "Basically, what we have established is that the more fit a player is, the greater a force it will take to injure him. This applies whether you're eight or eighty years old. The body is linked all together in a package. From our computers we get the complete picture, a profile. The brain, the heart, the spine, and the arms and legs are all examined and then we can draft the players who could probably sustain the contact in professional football."

EQUIPMENT

It takes more than just a football and a helmet to play the game. As the game gets more complicated, the equipment becomes more important, and today's football player is surrounded by specially designed padding, yards of adhesive tape, as well as other interesting tools of the trade.

All players wear various pads underneath their uniforms to absorb some of the shock. Running backs wear foam pads on their thighs to help reduce the injuries from the constant banging. Defensive players such as Doug Plank of the Chicago Bears also wear special pads. "I usually put two strips of foam rubber under my shoulder pads. But after I looked at the films of Earl Campbell, I stuck three strips in there."

Running back Wilbert Montgomery of the Philadelphia Eagles gets sore hands from being banged by the hard plastic helmets of the defense. He wears "sarancs," tight gloves made of deerskin, to protect his hands.

William Andrews of the Atlanta Falcons brings about 10 pairs of shoes to each game. He selects a pair depending upon the weather conditions and the type of playing surface (artificial or natural grass). The general rule is that frozen, hard turf requires short cleats and a wet field demands longer ones.

Obviously, the most important thing to a kicker is his leg, which must be protected. On the sideline, Atlanta Falcon punter John James wears an oversized insulated glove on his right foot to keep it warm. The placekicker for the Washington Redskins, Mark Moseley,

B arefooted Tony Franklin kicks another field goal for the Philadelphia Eagles.

wears five layers of socks on his kicking foot to get extra protection during the kick. (The Eagles' Tony Franklin, however, likes to kick barefooted!)

No player is as fragile as the quarterback, and many pieces of equipment have been developed to protect him. One of the most interesting is the flak jacket, which was invented by Byron Donzis and made popular by Dan Pastorini when he was with the Houston Oilers.

San Francisco's Steve DeBerg, suffering from a throat ailment, tries out the microphone taped to his helmet. A small amplifier enabled his signals to be heard by teammates.

Pastorini was in the hospital with broken ribs. Donzis came by and told him, "If you have this jacket on, I can hit you with a baseball bat and you won't feel anything." Donzis put the flak jacket on and had a friend crack him with a bat. Convinced, Pastorini wore the jacket as soon as he rejoined the Oilers. The jacket is designed to withstand direct hits to the ribs and kidneys from the front, back, or sides.

During the 1980 season, Steve De-Berg, who was the quarterback for the San Francisco 49ers, had almost lost his voice, so he was equipped with a special microphone and amplifier to help him call signals at the line of scrimmage. When Jets quarterback Richard Todd hurt his ribs the following year, raising his voice enough to be heard at the line of scrimmage was very painful, so the microphone and amplifier were sent to the Jets by the 49ers, and Todd wore them during some games.

CLOSING NOTES

The words of wisdom of the Super Athletes and coaches are extremely valuable. They come after years of experience; on the sideline and on the field, as well as on the telephone between games.

The learning process is long and tedious. The secrets of the Super Athletes should help guide any student of the game of football, much the same way that they aided the stars themselves.

"Practice makes perfect"—it's an old saying that every member of the NFL, from star quarterback to second-string ball boy, knows to be true.

QUIZ

Match the Players with Their Nicknames

1.	Crazylegs	a.	Don Meredith
2.	Bubba	b.	O. J. Simpson
3.	The Juice	c.	Richard Lane
4.	Dandy Don	d.	Jack Tatum
5.	Broadway Joe	e.	Charles Smith
6.	Bullet Bob	f.	Bob Hayes
7.	Night Train	g.	Elroy Hirsch
8.	The Deacon	h.	Joe Namath
9.	The Assassin	i.	Dave Jones

Who scored the most career touchdowns?

Answer: Jim Brown scored 126 touchdowns for the Cleveland Browns from 1957 to 1965.

What team has scored the most total points in Super Bowl play?

Answer: The Dallas Cowboys have appeared in five Super Bowls, scoring 112 points.

Who holds the record for most seasons played?

Answer: George Blanda played for 26 seasons as a placekicker and quarterback for the Chicago Bears, Baltimore Colts, Houston Oilers, and Oakland Raiders.

Who was the first defensive lineman ever to be named the Player of the Year by the Football Writers of America?

Answer: Alan Page of the Minnesota Vikings in 1971.

Who played on the Buffalo Bills' offensive line in 1973, when O.J. Simpson set the 2,003-yard season rushing record?

Answer: Center Bruce Jarvis, guards Joe DeLamielleure and Reggie McKenzie, and tackles Dave Foley and Donnie Green.

What quarterback holds the record for most consecutive passes attempted without an interception?

Answer: Bart Starr of the Green Bay Packers completed 294 passes without an interception between 1964 and 1965.

How far did the shortest touchdown pass travel?

Answer: Eddie LeBaron threw a touchdown pass two inches to Dick Bielski in a Dallas Cowboy –Washington Redskin game in 1960.

If you liked SECRETS OF THE SUPER ATHLETES: **Football**, don't miss the other books in this series:

★ Basketball by David Fremon
★ Baseball by Abbot Neil Solomon
★ Soccer by John Devaney

Get the inside line on the most popular sports in America today—straight talk and secret tips from the greatest players, the professional viewpoint from the coaches and managers of the champion teams, plus more action and more hard information than you can find in any other sports books.

All four books are packed with action photos of your favorite stars.

Be an all-round winner, a sports fan who knows what he's talking about, a player who knows how to win. Buy the entire series of SECRETS OF THE SUPER ATHLETES.